God in the Winter
13 Weekly Devotions & Bible Studies for Men

Jarome Davis
Mark Simmons

Valeece Simmons-Davis

Copyright © 2023 Valeece Simmons-Davis

All rights reserved

No part of this book may be reproduced, or stored in a retrieval system, or transmitted in any form or by any means, electronic, mechanical, photocopying, recording, or otherwise, without express written permission of the publisher.

Printed in the United States of America

This book is dedicated to all men who are chasing after God's own heart.

"Do not conform to the pattern of this world, but be transformed by the renewing of your mind. Then you will be able to test and approve what God's will is—his good, pleasing and perfect will."
Romans 12:2 NIV

CONTENTS

Title Page
Copyright
Dedication
Epigraph
Welcome

Week 1: Born Again	1
Week 2: A Better Resolution	5
Week 3: Real Men Wear Faith	9
Week 4: Lion Tamer	13
Week 5: Take Care of Home	18
Week 6: God Is bigger	22
Week 7: A Love Story	28
Week 8: Work Your Faith	32
Week 9: Word to the Wise	36
Week 10: Just Prosper	40
Week 11: When to Stand	44
Week 12: Acts of Love	48
Week 13: First Things First	51
See You Next Season	55
Books in This Series	57

Acknowledgements 59

WELCOME

Greetings Brother in Christ,

You are here for a reason. There is nothing like renewing yourself in the winter with the Lord as your guide. Maybe you would like to maintain your relationship with God by studying his word, or you may be new to the body of Christ, yearning for deeper knowledge. Regardless of your reason for picking up this book, know that God approves of your willingness to be an empty vessel for him. He will certainly pour into you. Get ready for the overflow.

This book has thirteen devotions and Bible studies for each week of winter. If you have a routine of studying the Bible, you are already on a great track and will certainly love these studies! Nonetheless, you will continue to increase your dependence on the Holy Spirit to teach you the word inductively. You do not have to fear not understanding the word if the Holy Spirit is your guide. Therefore, prayers are at the beginning and end of each study to ensure you have the presence of God with you. Make sure your heart's posture is toward him.

All God's children are responsible for seeking and knowing the word personally. Going to church on Sunday is not enough. Being faithful with small group Bible studies is a big win! However, there is nothing like knowing God's word for yourself. If you do not know the word personally, how are you equipping yourself against Satan's schemes? Don't forget that Satan knows the Bible, and he knows it well. God's children who are not familiar with the word are likely to be gullible and fall susceptible to cycles of sin. In the Holy Bible, we are called to present ourselves to God as approved workers who are not ashamed and who abide in God's truth (2 Timothy 2:15). Let's reiterate this point: If you do not know the word for yourself, you cannot discern the word of truth. Therefore, studying is a matter of life and death.

Next, here are some tips to help you prepare for your Bible study each week. The primary book you need is the Holy Bible. Any version will do. However, the verses used in this book will be in the New International Version (NIV). A study Bible is highly recommended. If you prefer to use other Bible study tools such as Bible dictionaries, commentaries, or credible online tools, such as blueletterbible.org, please use the resources to help clarify meaning and consolidate your learning. Furthermore, you can use credible online resources to review maps of regions.

Reread scriptures and do not skip cross-references that provide more insight. You want to take in all that God has to give you. The more knowledge you acquire to put scripture in the right context, the richer your Bible study will be. Finally, set aside at least 2 hours per week. Simply replace two hours when you may be watching TV or playing games on your phone with 2 hours of one-on-one with God.

This book is simply a guide to encourage you. Its purpose is to help you maintain a habit of studying the Bible as the leader of your home. You are the student, and the Holy Spirit is your teacher. Your curriculum is the Holy Bible! You will have confidence to go to any reading in the Bible and allow the Holy Spirit to teach you.

Because you stepped out on faith and made a commitment to study the word line by line, God will bless you. Through you, God will bless so many others. Your schedule may be busy but prioritize God because he is important. Set aside time for God because he makes time for you. He believes you are important, too.

Your Brothers in Christ,

Jarome and Mark

WEEK 1: BORN AGAIN

Key Question
Why did God send his son, and what does this mean to me?

Opening Prayer
　　Lord, you sent your one and only son. His earthly parents were Joseph and Mary who believed in you and were good stewards of Jesus as he grew up. Help me understand the profoundness of his birth and what Christ the living hope can do for me and the people I love. Help me have pure joy with my family and friends this holiday season by focusing on you. In the name of Jesus, Amen!

Devotion
　　The Christmas season is an uplifting holiday. Family and friends gather to soak in the merry atmosphere. People may seem a little happier and smile more. Still, what is the reason for this mood change in culture? Yes, Jesus was born to the virgin Mary a long time ago, but have people truly embraced the idea that Jesus is, indeed, the reason for the season.
　　The commercialization of Christmas can be a huge distraction for why we celebrate during this time of year. As we continue to age and acquire Godly wisdom, we should be cautious to revolve our season around Christmas lists and a spending budget. Do we like to give gifts and receive gifts? Absolutely! Nothing is wrong with gift giving. In fact, the Bible states it is better to give than to receive. Still, once we exchange gifts, then what? Be careful not to overcompensate with gifts due to guilt or attempt to fill a void. For example, some parents are guilty of replacing gifts with time. We think if we give our kids materialistic desires, then we are sufficient. The bottom line is that most people do not care about

expensive gifts, including children. They care more about the time spent with you.

In the book of Ecclesiastes, Solomon discusses the vanities of life, or the things in life which are meaningless. The glitz and glam of Christmas are vain. It is all vanity if Jesus is not in the center of your life during Christmas and throughout the entire year. Jesus should always be the heart of your home. If God isn't in all that you do, your Christmas holiday and life itself are vain.

As you enjoy Christmas with loved ones this year and exchange gifts, remember we celebrate the birth of God's son as our ultimate gift. Jesus was born to bring salvation to all mankind. Have you been "born again" in Christ and accepted him as your Lord and Savior? Jesus came for a reason. The reason is you! Therefore, do not forget to put Jesus first and model this for your family and friends. Proclaim the gospel! Share the good news of your salvation.

Key Verse

"For God so loved the world that he gave his one and only son, that whoever believes in him shall not perish but have eternal life."
John 3:16 NIV

Bible Study

    Read John 3:1-21.
    Who authored the book of John?
    Who is the author's initial audience?
    When was the book written?

    Look at John 3:1-9.

        How is Nicodemus described in verse 1? What else do you learn about him in John 7:50-51?

        What did Nicodemus say when he went to Jesus in verse 2? What do you learn from Acts 2:22-24 and Acts 10:38 that connects to verse 2?

        How did Jesus respond in verse 3?

What was the question Nicodemus asked next in verse 4? Did he understand what Jesus meant by being "born again"?

What did Jesus say in verses 5-8 to help the Pharisee understand? What else do you learn about being "born again" in Titus 3:5?

What did Nicodemus ask next in verse 9?

Look at John 3:10-15.
What does Jesus say in verse 10-15?
Read these cross-references for more insight about what Jesus was teaching Nicodemus. What does it teach you?
Luke 2:46
John 1:18; 6:38; 7:16-17; 8:28, 12:32
Proverbs 30:4
Acts 2:34

Look at John 3:16-21.
Why did God send Jesus as flesh to walk among us?

What happens to those who do not believe?

What is said about light and darkness? Why do people who do evil hate the light?

What is said about people who live by the truth?

What else do you learn from the cross-references that connect to the conversation between Jesus and Nicodemus?
Romans 5:8
Ephesians 2:4-5
John 1:4; 5:24 6:29, 40, 57; 8:12; 10:36; 11:42; 12:47; 17:8
1 John 4:9
Ephesians 5:11-13

Why did Jesus come? Did everyone believe back then? Does everyone believe now? Do you believe?

Read other cross-references, commentaries, or use other Bible study tools as needed to consolidate your learning.

Reflection
Why did God send his son, and what does this mean to me?

Closing Prayer
Lord Jesus, you came to save me. You did it because of love. There is no greater love! You bore a cross that was meant for me! This is love I cannot repay and will never repay even if I spent a lifetime trying. I realize that being born again is part of the journey to get into heaven. I must walk in truth to be in the light, not in darkness. I want to share this word with everyone I know. The gate to heaven is narrow, and the gate to destruction is wide. Help us believe and enter the narrow gate, Lord! Open the eyes of your children to seek you, repent, and do right in your sight. In the name of Jesus, Amen!

WEEK 2: A BETTER RESOLUTION

Key Question
How can I begin my new year with a fresh start about who Jesus is?

Opening Prayer
Father God, you gave us Jesus Christ as the ultimate sacrifice for our sins. As you bless me each year to carry out your will, help me recognize who you are and how I can have an outpour of blessings if I simply trust. This year I want to walk more faithfully than ever. I want to be an example to other men, women, and children for how to walk with Jesus. In the name of Jesus, Amen!

Devotion
In southern states, it can be difficult to distinguish the seasons. Many people who live in the south would explain that we may not have a true winter season. We are fortunate to have cold fronts every now and then. On rare occasions, God allows it to snow. Nonetheless, it is not uncommon to see people without jackets, wearing shorts, and wearing sandals. On the other hand, we will also see people dressed as if there is definitely a change in the season. They may have heavy jackets, layered clothing, winter hats, and winter boots. In this case, it is easier to recognize the change in seasons due to how people change up their clothes.

In the past, our parents and grandparents would have a conniption fit if they saw young children without a jacket on in the winter months. They still do have conniption fits! However, back in the day, if your parents or grandparents saw you without a jacket in the winter months, no matter the temperature, you and everyone around you were going to hear about it. The likelihood of disciplinary action against you was 100%.

When Jesus came down from heaven, many people did not recognize that the "season" had changed. They missed the opportunity for God to change their lives through Jesus, our Lord and Savior. As you read this study, soften your heart to receive the word of God. Make a new resolution to seek and recognize when God is trying to change your life for the better.

Key Verses
"In the beginning was the Word, and the Word was with God, and the Word was God. He was with God in the beginning."
John 1:1-2 NIV

Bible Study
Read John 1:1-14.
Who wrote the book of John?
Who was the author's original audience?
When was the book written?

Look at John 1:1-5.
What are these verses discussing? Who is the "Word"?

The word, in verse 2, was with whom in the beginning?

What was made by the Word and God in verse 3? Does this include the universe? Does this include the world and everything in it?

Review John 17:5 for more insight. Who is speaking in this verse? To whom is he speaking? Is the "Word" equal to God?

What is true about light and darkness according to verse 5? Who is the light?

Review these cross-references for more insight about the "Word".
Revelations 19:13

John 3:19-21; 5:26, 8:12, 11:25
1 John 1:2
Philippians 2:6
Genesis 1:1
1 Corinthians 8:6
Colossians 1:16

Look at John 1:6-8.
Who came to witness about the light so that all may believe? Review Matthew 3:1 for more insight.

Look at John 1:9-14.
In verse 9, who is the true light that gives light to everyone in the world?

Even though the light was in the world and made the world, what is true in verses 10-11? Who is the group of people mentioned as "his own"? Did everyone believe?

What is true about all who did receive in verses 12-13?

Review the cross-references for more insight.
Galatians 3:26; 4:4
Isaiah 49:6
If we are not children of God, then who is our father instead of God? Why is this significant?

Who made his dwelling among us in verse 14? What does it mean that we have seen "his glory"?
Review the cross-references for more insight.
1 John 2:8
Hebrews 1:2
John 3:6; 14:6
James 1:18

Who is Jesus? Is he equal to God?
Was the Holy Spirit also with God and Jesus in the beginning in Genesis 1:1? How do you know?

What is true for believers?
What is true for those who do not believe?
Why is it important to reflect the light of Jesus?

Read other cross-references, commentaries, or use other Bible study tools as needed to consolidate your learning.

Reflection
How can I begin my new year with a fresh start about who Jesus is?

Closing Prayer
Father God, thank you for sending Jesus who was the Word as flesh. When Jesus walked the earth, he was fully human and fully God. Jesus still lives! He has been with you since the beginning of time and is with you now. This year, help me see your glory. May your glory be revealed in me. Increase my faith so that I may believe in you and all your ways. This year I want to keep Jesus first in all that I do. I know that Jesus is all I need. In the name of Jesus, Amen!

WEEK 3: REAL MEN WEAR FAITH

Key Question
How can I demonstrate faith for the people I influence as a leader?

Opening Prayer
Sovereign Lord, I know I can trust your word. As I prepare to study, teach me how I can bless others by showcasing faith as a leader of my home and a leader in other settings. May the Holy Spirit teach me to apply the word. In the name of Jesus, Amen!

Devotion
In winter months, it is common to see an uptick in contagious illnesses such as the flu. Peak season for many illnesses exists during winter months. We do all we can to protect ourselves and ensure those who contract illnesses are getting well. Flu shots, doctor's visits, medication, and social distancing from family and friends are strategies we use. These actions mean well to prevent spreading illnesses or to help others heal from their illnesses.

Contrarily, some illnesses are not contagious. They may be chronic illnesses such as asthma, cancer, arthritis, sinusitis, diabetes, or heart disease. Some may feel like this is something that will never go away and needs constant treatment by a doctor. Doctors are placed here on earth for expertise, providing advice and the best treatment they can. However, have you also tried a little faith in Jesus?

We have a Lord and Savior in Jesus who heals. He doesn't have to be physically present for us to experience this healing, nor does it take much to receive this. When we have family members or people we love who are ill, we can intercede for them. Whether in this life or the next, God is a healer. All it takes is an act of faith to ask God for healing!

Key Verse
"Then Jesus said to the centurion, 'Go! Let it be done just as you believed it would.' And his servant was healed at that moment.
Matthew 8:13 NIV

Bible Study
Read Matthew 8:5-13.
Who wrote the book of Matthew?
Who is the author's original audience?
When was the book written?

Look at Matthew 8:5-13.
Where was Jesus in verse 5? Who asked Jesus for help? What is true about this man's occupation?

What did the man say in verse 6?

How did Jesus respond in verse 7?

What did the man say to Jesus in verses 8-9? Did the centurion view Jesus as a man with authority?

Did Jesus come for Jews and Gentiles? Why is this significant? Did all Jews believe in Jesus even though they were his chosen people?

Review the cross-references for more insight.
Psalms 107:20
Matthew 15:28
Can Jesus heal from a distance?

What did Jesus say to the man in verse 10-12?

Review the cross-references for more insight.
Psalms 107:2-3

Isaiah 49:12; 59:19
Malachi 1:11
Luke 13:29
Matthew 13:38-42
Matthew 22:13; 24:51; 25:30
Luke 13:28

How does the reading end in verse Matthew 8:13? Did it take a long time for the servant to be healed? Was Jesus near the servant? How do you believe the servant felt?

What does this reading tell you about the centurion's faith and the servant who was suffering? What does this reading tell you about the power of Jesus and why he came to earth?

What will happen to those who do not believe?

Do you believe one man's act of faith can bless another man? Why or why not?

When you are in a position to lead by faith, how can you apply what you learned in this Bible reading?

Read other cross-references, commentaries, or use other Bible study tools as needed to consolidate your learning.

Reflection
How can I demonstrate faith for the people I influence as a leader?

Closing Prayer
  Sovereign Lord, you are God all by yourself. Help me have the faith of the centurion. He was a leader, a man with authority. However, the centurion knew a man with greater authority than he possessed. The man with authority from God the Father was Jesus Christ. Jesus had power that could reach any distance, and the centurion recognized this power. Lord, remind me of the power that lies in Jesus. Remind me that this is the same power that lives in me if I receive Jesus with my whole heart. I can lead others and be a blessing to others due to my act of faith. My

demonstration of faith shows that I want to be obedient to the words in the Holy Bible. Refine my walk and build my influence of faith for the people in my circle. In the name of Jesus, Amen!

WEEK 4: LION TAMER

Key Question
How does God intervene for me when others try to condemn me for walking faithfully with God?

Opening Prayer
   Dear God, as I try to walk faithfully with you and draw closer to you, I know there will be people and trials that try to thwart my walk. Distractions will try to take my focus off you. Show me how you intervened for Daniel, a man of faith. Increase my trust so that I will remain obedient to your word. Help me earn favor with people in powerful places who can help spread your word. In the name of Jesus, Amen!

Devotion
   Who doesn't love a good fire in the wintertime? Whether you have an electric fireplace or a traditional fireplace, the warmth of fire hitting you and your family on a cold, cold day is priceless. You feel safe and warm. Your family feels secure because they have shelter from the harsh weather outside.
   Think about the warmth and blessings that come to you when you are faithful in the word of God. While you elevate God's name, God also elevates you on your job, and overall, in your life. In the workplace, we may work with people who are not believers. It can be difficult because of jealousy or pure ignorance. You simply won't fit in. Don't try to fit in! When God puts a light in you, it will occupy the space of all darkness. For some people on your job, this is a threat, especially if your supervisor begins to favor you over others.
   Satan realizes his usual tactics will not work on you when you

are leveling up in God, so he sows seeds of darkness in others to put out your fire, your light. Sometimes, God's light will create darkness in others who have hardened their hearts. Simply put, these people do not like the light. The source controlling them is Satan. When issues like this arise, we cannot turn our back on the Lord. If anything, the trials that come further exhibit why we must remain faithful. The testing of our faith produces perseverance.

Still, some people yearn for more light! They recognize the God in you and your light spills over to them, influencing them to be better and walk faithfully. This is why you cannot give up. God sees you. He sees every trial, every tussle, every struggle. Remember, he has not left you. There is so much more in store for you and the people who are led by you.

Therefore, as you read about Daniel's situation, remember the unmatched warmth and the light of God. He always fulfills his promises and takes care of his own.

Key Verse
"My God sent his angel, and he shut the mouths of the lions. They have not hurt me, because I was found innocent in his sight."

Daniel 6:22 NIV

Bible Study
Read Daniel 6.
Who wrote the book of Daniel?
Who was the author's original audience?
When was the book written?

Look at Daniel 6:1-5.

> Who is Darius and what did he do in verse 1? Who was to rule throughout the kingdom? How many were to rule?

> Who was Daniel in verse 2?

> What happened in verse 3? What had Daniel done to win the king's favor? What does this say about the quality of Daniel's work?

Review the cross-references for more insight.
Genesis 41:41-42
Esther 10:3
Daniel 5:12-14
Who else has found favor with kings who did not believe in God?

What happened in verse 4? What was true about the other administrators and local rulers?

What did the men say in verse 5? Review Acts 24:13-16 for more insight. What is true about Daniel?

Look at Daniel 6:6-9.
What happened in verse 6-8? What was the plan against Daniel?

What did the king do in verse 9?

Review the cross-references for more insight.
Daniel 3:2-6
Psalms 59:3-4; 64:2-9
How do these verses relate to Daniel's situation?

Look at Daniel 6:10-16.
What did Daniel do in verse 10? Did he change his routine? Why or why not?

Review the cross-references for more insight.
1 Kings 8:48-49
Psalms 95:6
Acts 5:29

Why should we worship and obey God instead of humans?

What happened in verses Daniel 6:11-16?

How did the king feel in verse 14? What did he try to do? Why do you believe he felt this way? Let the Holy Spirit guide you.

What did the men do in verse 15?

What order was given in verse 16 and by whom? What did the king say to Daniel?

Look at Daniel 6:17-28.

What happened in verse 17? Could this situation change?

What did the king do in verse 18? Why do you believe he could not sleep? Let the Holy Spirit guide you.

What did the king do in verse 19?

What did the king do in verse 20? Why do you believe he was in anguish?

What did Daniel say in verses 21-22? How did the king feel in verse 23? What orders did he give? What was Daniel's condition?

What happened in verse 24? What happened before they reached the floor of the den? What does this tell you about men who are not following God? Who else can be hurt in the family when a man is not led by God?

What did King Darius do in verse 25?

Why do you feel the king was compelled to issue such a decree in verse 26?

What does the pagan king mention about the living God in verses 26-27? Was the king influenced by Daniel and the power of God?

How does the reading end in verse 28?

What does this tell you about Daniel's faith in God despite the initial decree? What does this tell you about Daniel's ability to influence the pagan king?

How does the light of God continue to shine despite plans of the enemy?

Read other cross-references, commentaries, or use other Bible study tools as needed to consolidate your learning.

Reflection

How does God intervene for me when others try to condemn me for walking faithfully with God?

Closing Prayer

Dear God, thank you for showing me your power to shut the mouths of lions if I am thrown into a lion's den. Daniel showed courage and prayed out to you even though it was against the king's decree. If I elevate you, I will be elevated with you because that is how good you are. Continue to let my light shine and lead others to the light, which is you. In the name of Jesus, Amen!

WEEK 5: TAKE CARE OF HOME

Key Question
How does the Christian household look? What is my role as the man of the house?

Opening Prayer
Gracious Father, thank you for being my guide. If I keep my focus on you, you will guide my footsteps to lead my household through all ups and downs. You call for consistency with obedience in my life. Help me see clearer how to lead the members of my home and do your will. In the name of Jesus, Amen!

Devotion
Valentine's Day is near, and the stores are full of items for loved ones to purchase gifts. However, what shows love greater than a gift? Action. People's daily behavior illustrates love. We sacrifice a lot for the people we love. This includes time, money, and putting our desires or needs on the back burner for others.

God showed us love when he sent his son to die on the cross for our sins. In fact, the Bible mentions that there is no greater love than a man who lays his life down for his friend. That's love! With this in mind, what does the Bible say about how a man runs a Christian household? What are the roles, and what does this look like? As Jesus is the head of the church, so is a man the head of his home. As you prepare for this study, think about the sacrifices of Jesus and how you can mirror this as you lead family members in your home.

Key Verse
"Husbands, love your wives just as Christ loved the church and

gave himself up for her..."

Ephesians 5:25 NIV

Bible Study
Read Ephesians 5:21-6:4.
Who wrote the book of Ephesians?
Who is the author's original audience?
When was the book written?

Look at Ephesians 5:21-27.
In verse 21, who should submit to whom and how?

How should wives submit to their husbands in verse 22? Why?

Who is the head of the wife in verse 23? In what manner should the head of the wife act? Is this a tall order?

Who submits to Christ in verse 24? How should the woman submit to her husband?

How should husbands love their wives in verses 25-27? Why?

Review the cross-references for more insight.
Galatians 5:13
Genesis 3:16
1 Corinthians 11:3
Ephesians 1:4, 22
Colossians 1:22; 3:19

Look at Ephesians 5:28-33.
In verses 28-30, how should men love their wives? Should a man love his wife in the same manner as Christ loves the members of his body, the church?

Why is verse 31 important? Think about one flesh. Which spouse represents the head? Which spouse represents the body?

What does Paul say in verse 32?

How does Ephesians 5 end in verse 33?

Review the cross-references for more insight.
Genesis 2:24
1 Corinthians 12:27
Matthew 19:5

Look at Ephesians 6:1-6:4

What should children do in verses 1-3? Why?

What is the warning to fathers in verse 4? What does the Bible say to do instead?

Who is responsible for leading the training and instruction of children in the Lord?

Review the cross-references for more insight.
Colossians 3:20-21
Exodus 20:12
Genesis 18:19
Deuteronomy 6:4-9

If a husband is faithful with the word of Christ, how will this impact the wife and children?

If a woman is to submit to her husband as the church body submits to Christ, what does this say about expectations for the husband's character?

What could be consequences for a household in which the wife submits to a husband who is not led by God? What is at risk? Are future generations at stake?

Should the man's home be his first ministry?

Read other cross-references, commentaries, or use other Bible study tools as needed to consolidate your learning.

Reflection

How does the Christian household look? What is my role as the man of the house?

Closing Prayer

Gracious Father, I see that being a husband is indeed a sacred role. The good news is that all husbands have you as a guide. Husbands who truly want to do right by their families will be sufficient because you are sufficient for them and their households. May husbands walk boldly in leadership as Christians who are refining themselves and sacrificing for their wives as Christ sacrificed for the church.

God shine your light on men who are engaged to be married so they may lead their marriages in lockstep with you. For broken marriages, I ask that you guide husbands on next steps according to your will. Heal husbands, wives, and children of broken marriages, Lord.

I know if men live in the ways of Christ, that members in their households will be influenced to be obedient and walk faithfully, too. Future generations will be blessed because husbands operate under Christ's authority. Lord impress upon men's hearts to lead and chase you. So much is at stake. In the name of Jesus, Amen!

WEEK 6: GOD IS BIGGER

Key Question
In what ways can I show courage throughout my life knowing God fights my battles for me?

Opening Prayer
   God Almighty, your strength is amazing. You go before me and stand behind me through every test and trial. Thank you for fighting my battles for me. Show me how I can be courageous like the shepherd boy David who seemed to be an unlikely hero in a time of desperation. Manifest your will for my life as I turn my heart towards you and learn about David's courage. In the name of Jesus, Amen!

Devotion
   If you ever studied ants, you know something about them. To say they are small little creatures, they are STRONG! Have you ever witnessed ants carry food particles that were on the ground? Traveling in a line, one by one the food is taken back to the ant colony somewhere in the ground to store for later.
   In winter, some ant colonies are deep enough in the soil, so they are shielded from winter weather. On average, these little critters can carry about 10 to 50 times their weight. Certain types of ants can carry up to 4,000 times their weight. This is truly an act of God that we take for granted and do not ponder. If the average human had the strength of an ant, they could lift a small car. Imagine that! However, the world's strongest person can only lift about 2.5 times his body weight.
   If you think about the power in a little bitty ant, created by God himself, to take on food that is 50 times its size, what makes you

think the same God who created you, cannot help you carry heavy burdens? The problem may be large in your eyes, but it is a matter of a spoken word from God to have your burden removed. You just have to believe. As you read about Daniel's victory, think about the power of calling on God's name.

Key Verse
"David said to the Philistine, 'You come against me with sword and spear and javelin, but I come against you in the name of the Lord Almighty, the God of the armies of Israel, whom you have defied.'"

1 Samuel 17:45 NIV

Bible Study
Read 1 Samuel 17.
Who wrote the book of 1 Samuel?
Who was the author's original audience?
When was it written?

Look at 1 Samuel 17:1-3
Who gathered for war and where did they assemble in verse 1?

In verse 2, who assembled and where did they assemble? With whom were they at war? Who is the leader of this group?

In verse 3, what was between the two opposing sides who occupied hills? Was this an intense moment? Describe the setting and tension.

Look at the cross-references for more insight.
Isaiah 13:4-5, 21:9
2 Chronicles 28:18

Look at 1 Samuel 17:4-7.
Who is Goliath? Where was he from? Which side was he on?

How tall was Goliath? Describe what he wore. Does he seem

intimidating to his opponents? Why or why not?

Look at the cross-references for more insight.
Joshua 11:21-22
2 Samuel 21:19

Look at 1 Samuel 17:8-11.
What does Goliath say in verses 8-10?

What was the feeling of the Israelites in verse 11? Was the leader concerned?

Look at 1 Samuel 17:12-24.
Who was David and Jesse in verse 12? Where was Jesse from? How many sons did Jesse have?

Which sons followed Saul to the war in verse 13?
Which son was the youngest in verse 14?
What did David have to do in verse 15?

In verse 16, what happened each morning and evening? For how long? Think about the positions of the armies and the valley in between. Was there great risk for casualties and a disadvantage of trying to fight uphill? Let the Holy Spirit guide you.

Review the cross-references for more insight.
Ruth 4:17
1 Chronicles 2:13-15
Genesis 25:19
1 Samuel 16:8-23

What did Jesse tell his son David in verses 17-19? Why?
What did David do in verse 20?
What was happening at the time in verse 21?
What did David do in verse 22?
What happened in verses 22 and 23?
What did the Israelites do when they saw Goliath in verse 24?

Look at 1 Samuel 17:25-40.
What will happen to the man who kills Goliath in verse 25?
What did David ask in verse 26?
How did the men respond in verse 27?

What did David's oldest brother say in verse 28? How was his brother feeling at the time?

How did David respond to his brother in verse 29?
What did David do in verse 30?

Review the cross-references for more insight.
Joshua 15:16
1 Samuel 18:17
Genesis 37:4
Proverbs 18:19
Matthew 10:36
How do each of these cross-references connect to the current reading?

Who sent for David in verse 31? Why?
What did David say to Saul in verse 32?
What did Saul say in verse 33? Was this encouraging or not?

How did David respond in verses 34-37? Did David seem confident or discouraged? How did he perceive Goliath as opposed to Saul and others in the Israelite army?

What did Saul say at the end of verse 37?
How did Saul try to prepare David in verse 38-39?
What did David say and do in verse 39?

What did David do in verse 40? Can you imagine this moment? Think for a minute. Let the Holy Spirit guide you.

Review the cross-references for more insight.
Deuteronomy 20:3
Numbers 13:31
Jeremiah 49:19

Amos 3:12
2 Chronicles 1:10
2 Timothy 4:17
1 Chronicles 22:11-13
What do you learn from these verses?

Look at 1 Samuel 17:41-47.

What did Goliath, the Philistine, do in verses 41-44? How did Goliath feel about David? Why? Who did he curse David by?

How did David speak in verses 45-47? Did he speak with courage or fear?

Who did David give credit concerning his future victory in verse 46?

What did David say in verse 47? What does this tell you about David's faith?

Review the cross-references for more insight.
Psalms 123:3-4; 124:8
Proverbs 16:18
2 Samuel 22:33-35
1 Kings 18:36-37
2 Kings 19:19
2 Chronicles 32:8
Deuteronomy 28:25-26
Joshua 4:24
Isaiah 37:20; 52:10
Hosea 1:7
Zechariah 4:6

Should you fear a battle if you come in the name of the Lord? If not, who should be fearful?

Look at 1 Samuel 17:48-58.

What happened in verse 48? Is this a critical moment concerning the war?

What did David do in verse 49? What happened as a result?
What happened in verses 50-51? What did the Philistines do?
How did events of the battle change in verse 52?
What happened in verses 53-54?

Who is talking in verses 55-56? Describe the conversation.
Who brought David before Saul? When did he take him? What did David have with him?
What did Saul say to David in verse 58? How did David respond?

What do David's actions tell you about his trust in God?
How did David impact the Israelites the day he killed Goliath? Was this a big deal?

Review the cross-references for more insight.
2 Samuel 23:21
Hebrew 11:32-34

Read other cross-references, commentaries, or use other Bible study tools as needed to consolidate your learning.

Reflection
In what ways can I show courage throughout my life knowing God fights my battles for me?

Closing Prayer
God Almighty, I praise you for my future victories. Lord, I will always remember that you fight for me. I never have to be afraid. I do not fear my future because I serve an all-powerful God. Your ways are higher than my ways. You came through for a shaken Israelite army in a time of fear. However, you chose David as a hero for the Israelites. David had a bag of stones, Lord. However, you were the power behind David. He came in your name. When I come in your name, I know you fight my battles. You win every time. In Jesus name, Amen!

WEEK 7: A LOVE STORY

Key Question
How can couples in Christ reflect their love for each other from God's perspective?

Opening Prayer
God, you have a perfect plan for married couples who live by your word. May all married couples and couples engaged to be married reflect your love. When a man finds a wife, he finds someone special. Together, a husband and wife can do so much for God's kingdom, and they can reflect Christ's love for the church. As I prepare to read your holy word, help me understand the ways a man should feel about his wife or wife-to-be in your eyes. May all men seek your word concerning courtship and love in their marriages. In the name of Jesus, Amen!

Devotion
The month of February is upon us, and some people go all out for Valentine's Day. They want to make their loved ones feel special and appreciated. However, such love should not be expressed just on Valentine's Day, on birthdays, or on other holidays. Couples in Christ show such love ongoingly to maintain a strong marriage throughout the years.

Courtship is such a fun time for couples. However, sometimes that spark and passion dwindle when husbands and wives get distracted with everyday tasks such as work schedules, kids, school, or unexpected events. Unfortunately, some couples seek desires outside of marriage, which is unhealthy. Remember, Satan will do everything he can to tear marriages apart. The choice is up to each individual within each couple to not fall for Satan's schemes. Spouses must focus on God and each other. Spouses should pray for each other, pray together, and study the word together. God is the tie that keeps couples together. Sin is what leads to broken marriages and divorce.

God instituted marriage to uphold how Christ loves his church. Not only does God showcase how Christ loves the church in his word, but he is such a loving God that he mentions the beauty of love between a husband and wife in his word as well. As you think about marriage, think about how God's word guides married couples and engaged couples to never stop loving each other. Couples must create the time and space to discuss the goodness of God and maintain their marriage by letting each other know how special they are in words and in actions.

Key Verse
"You are altogether beautiful, my darling; there is no flaw in you."
Song of Songs 4:7 NIV

Bible Study
Read Song of Songs 4:1-5:1.
Who wrote the book Song of Songs?
Who is the author's original audience?
When was the book written?
Why was the book written?

Look at Song of Songs 4:1-7.
Who is speaking in these verses?
How does the man begin this reading?

How are the woman's eyes, hair, teeth, lips, and temples described in verses 1-3? Why were such analogies used in those days? Let the Holy Spirit guide you.

Read the cross-references for more insight.
Micah 7:14
Song of Songs 5:12,16
Song of Songs 6:5-7

How are the woman's features described in verses 4-5?

Review the cross-references for more insight.
Song of Songs 2:16; 6:2-3; 7:3-4
Ezekiel 27:10
Proverbs 5:19

What else does the man say in verse 6?
How does the man describe his bride in verse 7?

Review the cross-references for more insight.
Song of Songs 1:15; 2:17

Look at Song of Songs 4:8-15.
What does the man say to his bride in verse 8?
How has the woman stolen his heart in verse 9?
How does he describe the woman's love in verse 10?
How does he describe the woman's lips and fragrance in verse 11?

How does he use a garden to describe the woman in verses 12-15? Can you imagine such a garden in those days? How would love like this make a man feel? Is his woman a refreshing woman or a woman who drains him?

Review the cross-references for more insight.
Genesis 41:42
Song of Songs 1:2,12,14; 3:6, 6:11; 7:6,12
Psalms 19:10
Hosea 14:6
Proverbs 5:15-18
Exodus 30:23

How do the cross-references connect to the reading?

Look at Song of Songs 4:16.
Who is speaking in this verse?
What does the woman say about her beloved concerning her garden?

Is she in love? How does the man make her feel?

Look at Song of Songs 5:1
What does the man say in verse 1? How does he feel about the love of his bride and "her garden"?

Who is speaking in the very last sentence of the verse? Are they happy for the couple?

Review the cross-references for insight.
Song of Songs 2:3
Isaiah 55:1-3

How does the bride and groom feel about each other? Do they hesitate to share how they feel? How does God show couples he is all they need?

Read other cross-references, commentaries, or use other Bible study tools as needed to consolidate your learning.

Reflection
How can couples in Christ reflect their love for each other from God's perspective?

Closing Prayer
God, thank you for revealing the beauty of love between a husband and wife through your poetic word. I pray couples who are not in Christ turn to Christ. For the married couples and couples in courtship who are in Christ, I pray they stay committed to Christ as individuals. My prayer is that you strengthen marriages all over the world, helping them to reflect your perfect love. Healthy marriages in Christ beget healthy children in Christ. May God bless generations of believers and healthy marriages. In the name of Jesus, Amen!

WEEK 8: WORK YOUR FAITH

WORK YOUR FAITH

Key Question
How do I exercise my faith as a believer in Christ?

Opening Prayer
Gracious God, thank you for another opportunity to do your will. You never leave me nor forsake me. You empower me to do right, not wrong. Show me how to truly exercise my faith as a believer and consult you as I live my life. Help me be obedient to your word. Equip me with the tools I need. In the name of Jesus, Amen!

Devotion
It is over half-way through the winter season. In the upper half of the U.S., people are likely enjoying super cold temperatures, snow, and all things that epitomize a beautiful winter season during this time of year. In the Southern U.S., however, you will likely get a little bit of everything! You may get spring-like weather one day, winter weather with snow a couple days, back to spring-like weather for a few days, and then, freezing rain the next day. Eventually, the weather patterns will level out, and spring will appear! No matter the weather patterns in your region of the U.S or the world, one thing is for certain, God shows us evidence that he exists, and he is in charge of the weather.

Think about the intentionality of God when he created the seasons. We can live out an entire year and noticeably see and feel the changes in the weather that created the seasons winter, spring, summer, and fall. Just as God shows us in so many ways that he is God and God alone, we can show people what walking in faith truly looks like. This would help people who struggle with their faith in God and nonbelievers who are in search of healing. This is so important because if nonbelievers see Christians who claim to have faith but do not show any evidence, or receipts, of said faith, how do we bring people to Christ? Start with the fundamentals. For example, do you pray and study the word of God consistently for yourself? When you hear from God, are you obedient? Do you listen?

Prepare yourself for great examples of what working your faith can be like in your everyday life.

Key Verse
"But someone will say, 'You have faith; I have deeds.' Show me your faith without deeds, and I will show you my faith by my deeds."
James 2:18 NIV

Bible Study
Read James 2:14-26.
Who wrote the book of James?
Who is the author's original audience?
When was the book written?

Look at James 2:14-19.
What is the question in verse 14 concerning faith and deeds?
What situation is mentioned in verse 15?
What is the question posed in verse 16?
What is the point the author makes in verse 17?

Review the cross-references for more insight.
Matthew 25: 34-40
James 1:22-25
1 John 3:17-18

What does the author go on to say in verse 18? How does the author reiterate his point?

What does the author say in verse 19? Why does the author say this?

Review the cross-references for more insight.
Romans 3:28-31
James 3:13-18
Deuteronomy 6:4
Matthew 8:29
Luke 4:34

Does the Devil know God's power? Do you know God's power? If people don't "work their faith," will they really experience the power of God?

Look at James 2:20-26.
What is the question posed in verse 20?
What example does the author use in verse 21 to discuss an exemplar of faith?

How was Abraham's faith made complete based on verse 22?
What does the author say in verse 23?

How does the author, once again, connect faith and action in verse 24?

What example does the author use in verse 25 to illustrate faith?

In verse 26, how does the author compare the body and the spirit to faith without works?

Review these cross-references for more insight.
Genesis 15:6, 22:9-14
Hebrew 11
1 Thessalonians 1:2-3
Romans 4:3
Isaiah 41:8-10

What is the bottom-line concerning faith and works? Does your faith have evidence? Does your life bear good fruit?

Read other cross-references, commentaries, or use other Bible study tools as needed to consolidate your learning.

Reflection
How do I exercise my faith as a believer in Christ?

Closing Prayer
Gracious God, thank you for showing me examples of faith in your word as demonstrated by Abraham and Rahab. Help me work my faith each day of my life. God, show me who I should help and how I should work for your kingdom. If I should pray for a cause or someone, tell me. If I should give time to a cause or help someone, show me. If I have resources and talents that I need to use for your will, show me how to align my resources and time so that I may work my faith in a manner that is pleasing to you. I understand that you recognize and approve of even the smallest acts of obedience. In the name of Jesus, Amen!

WEEK 9: WORD TO THE WISE

Key Question
Why should I be diligent to discern Godly wisdom and live a righteous life?

Opening Prayer
Precious Lord, your word never fails me. I yearn to learn more about you. I want to choose you every day. Renew my spirit. Each day I live on this earth is an opportunity for me to breathe in your word and live out your word. I know the strategies of Satan are to have people go astray. However, the power of you that lies in me is stronger than Satan. Therefore, I choose you every day, and I have no business giving focus to an enemy who is already defeated. Clean up my heart, Lord, so I may receive all you have in the study that lies ahead of me. In the name of Jesus, Amen!

Devotion
If you truly have an appreciation for nature and the way God created animals, you can see the beauty in how animals use instincts to live abundant lives. For example, bears hibernate in the winter and come out in the spring. Some animals ensure they have safe shelter and store up food before the winter months. This ensures they are warm, safe, and have food for them and their young. Turn your attention to household animals such as dogs. Dogs have instincts that one would deem wise. For example, if dogs sense danger or something that they feel needs attention, they bark and notify the owner.

God teaches us many lessons through how he created animals. Primarily, he teaches us and guides us to be wise through his word. If we are wise in our own ways versus God's ways, we set ourselves up for an inevitable end of darkness and spiritual death. No one in their right mind wants that. However, selfish ambitions and giving in to fleshly desires blinds us from the truth of God. Therefore, open your heart to seek God's ways and not your own. All that will be left from chasing sin is suffering and loneliness. Instead, choose God's way of longevity and spiritual prosperity because you choose to be wise in his eyes.

Key Verse
The fear of the Lord is the beginning of knowledge, but fools despise wisdom and instruction.
Proverbs 1:7 NIV

Bible Study
    Read Proverbs 1.
    Who wrote the book of Proverbs?
    Who is the author's original audience?
    When was the book written?

    Look at verses Proverbs 1:1-7.
        Who is Solomon?
        How do these verses outline the purpose of the book of Proverbs?
        What is the purpose in verse 1?
        What is the purpose in verse 2?
        What is the purpose in verse 3?
        What is the purpose in verse 4?
        What is the purpose in verse 5?
        What is the purpose in verse 6?

    Does the book of Proverbs cater to all people, all age groups, and to people at various levels of wisdom?

    Review the cross-references for more insight.
    1 Kings 4:29-34
    Proverbs 2:10-11; 8:12-13; 9:9-10; 15:33
    Psalms 49:3-4; 78:1-4; 111:10

Job 28:28
Ecclesiastes 12:13

Look at Proverbs 1:8-19.
What is the instruction given to sons in verse 8?
How are the teachings of parents described in verse 9?

What is the warning to sons in verses 10-15? Why? Does this message only apply to sons or can it apply to daughters, too?

What is true about the ways of men in verses 16-19?

What happens to such people who go after wrongful gain? Is this the work of Satan?

Review the cross-references for more insight.
Proverbs 4:1-9,14; 15:27; 16:29
Deuteronomy 13:6-8
Psalms 1:1; 10:8; 119:101

Look at Proverbs 1:20-33.
Who is calling out in verse 20-21? What is being said?

Where is wisdom making the "speech"? Is "wisdom" trying to get people's attention?

What is asked in verse 22?
What is the call to action in verse 23?

What will wisdom do and what happens to people who do not listen to the voice of wisdom in verses 24-27?

After disaster strikes, what does "wisdom" go on to say in verse 28?

Why does "wisdom" say those who did not listen and had disaster fall upon them will not find her? See verses 29-30.

What happens to people who do not heed to the voice of wisdom from the Lord in verses 31-32?

What is the comfort and security for those who do listen to wisdom in verse 33?

Review the cross-references for more insight.
Isaiah 65:12; 66:4
Jeremiah 7:13; 11:11
Micah 3:4
Zechariah 7:11, 13
Psalms 81:11
Ezekiel 8:18
Job 4:8; 21:14

What happens if we do not listen to wisdom's call?

Read other cross-references, commentaries, or use other Bible study tools as needed to consolidate your learning.

Reflection
Why should I be diligent to discern Godly wisdom and live a righteous life?

Closing Prayer
Precious Lord, just as you granted Soloman wisdom when he asked, grant me wisdom. Guide me and assist me with discerning your voice from the voice of Satan. I do not desire to pursue the desires of my flesh for the end is not good for anyone who does not heed the voice of Godly wisdom. Therefore, I will commit to hearing your voice, reading your word, and seeking your instruction so that I will not be simple-minded. Help me be prudent and give me discernment. In the name of Jesus, Amen!

WEEK 10: JUST PROSPER

Key Question
What does the Psalmist say about the company we keep? What shall I do to prosper and remain in God's will?

Opening Prayer
  Father God, if I am in you. I will live and not die. I will be faithful and bear good fruit because you lead me. Reveal the concepts you need me to understand for this week's study. May the Holy Spirit teach me your ways and open my eyes to see from your perspective. Put me in circles of God-fearing, like-minded people who are on fire to do your will and live a life for you. In the name of Jesus, Amen!

Devotion
  You have heard the saying that "birds of a feather flock together," right? Jesus was the only person who could walk and sit with sinners and, not even in the least, be seduced by sin. Although Jesus was fully human, the fact remains he was fully God. Therefore, in no way shape or form, could Jesus be persuaded to do wrong. He was without sin! This, however, does not hold true for mankind.
  Before winter, certain bird species in the Northern U.S. fly to the Southern U.S. to warmer regions. Their instincts kick in, signaling that it is time to fly south. When things seem to warm up in the north and get hotter in the south, their instincts kick in again. Then, these flocks of birds fly back north. It would be very strange to see diverse birds in one flock. Hence, the old saying "birds of a feather flock together."
  Whether you want to hear it or not, this is true for men

and women. The company you keep is what you feed yourself knowingly or subconsciously. Think about your family, friends, social media feeds, what you watch on TV, the music you enjoy, and the apps that consume your time on your smart devices. Does all this align to God's word? Which aspects need work?

Believe it or not, there are higher heights we can climb in God. Some people stay in the infant stages of Christianity for a very long time. It is easy to revert to sinful ways. There are examples in the Bible where faithful people fell to sin. Those examples are in the Bible for a reason.

Some of us need to "climb higher" in Christ. In what ways is God calling you to level up and prosper? We cannot obtain all that God has for us if we are content in our current state. There is so much more God can give us if we seek him diligently.

Key Verses
"Blessed is the one who does not walk in step with the wicked or stand in the way that sinners take or sit in the company of mockers, but whose delight is in the law of the Lord, and who meditates on his law day and night."

Psalm 1:1-2 NIV

Bible Study
Read Psalm 1.
Who wrote the book of Psalms?
Who is the author's original audience?
When was the book written?

Look at Psalm 1:1-6.
How does verse 1 begin?

In verse 2, what does a person who is blessed by the Lord do?

What is such a person compared to in verse 3?

What is the blessing for a person who stays clear of wicked people at the end of verse 3?

Review the cross-references for more insight.

Proverbs 4:14
Jeremiah 15:17
Psalms 26:4; 119:1, 16, 35; 128:3
Joshua 1:8
Jeremiah 17:18
Ezekial 47:12
Genesis 39:3
Isaiah 17:13
How does each verse connect to the reading?

How does the reading change its mood in verse 4? What are the wicked like?

What will happen to the wicked and sinners in verse 5?

How does this Psalm end? Who does God watch over? Where does the path for the wicked lead them?

Review the cross-references for more insight.
Psalms 5:5; 9:7; 37:18
2 Timothy 2:19

Read other cross-references, commentaries, or use other Bible study tools as needed to consolidate your learning.

Reflection
What does the Psalmist say about the company we keep? What shall I do to prosper and remain in God's will?

Closing Prayer
Father God, your word is truth. The word says if I meditate on you day and night and read your word, I will prosper in all I do, not whither. Help me yearn for more of your word. Help me be diligent about praying and seeking you. May my goals align with your goals. May the company I keep align with righteous people who can sharpen me. I am never too far gone that you cannot reach me, neither am I too righteous that I cannot continue to improve. You are a God of wisdom, humility, grace, and strength. Show me your glory, Lord. Work in me so I may prosper and have overflow for

those in my circle to prosper as well. In the name of Jesus, Amen!

WEEK 11: WHEN TO STAND

Key Question
How can I recognize when I need to stand up for God's truth?

Opening Prayer
Almighty God, your ways are perfect. If I abide in your truth, you abide in me. Give me the confidence and competence to speak up for your truth when I am called to do so. Help me hold my tongue in times when you have told me to wait. Lord, chasing you is awesome. Your love is unfailing. Your grace is enough for me. Lead me. Teach me in this study by providing an example of what standing up for you looks like. In the name of Jesus, Amen!

Devotion
God created the world and everything in it. Even though we were beautifully and wonderfully made by him, our choices to choose sin separates us from him. When we are making good choices aligned with God, we must be diligent about seeking guidance and being consistent. It is easy to be led astray if your guard is down.

Suppose a referee calls a high school championship basketball game. It's the end of the season, so there is a lot at stake! If the head referee shows any favoritism, he could certainly alter the outcome of a close game. If he leads his fellow referees to make unfair calls or show the slightest bit of favoritism towards one team, it could make the opposing team lose faith. If this is the case, basically, the opposing team will play the game in vain. All the referees need to do is follow the rule book and make the game fair for both teams. No harm, no foul.

As you approach this Bible study, think about God's work and doing things "by the book." When we deviate from the word in the smallest ways, it makes a great impact. Our influence can lead other followers astray, and we will have to answer to God for causing other people to stumble. Therefore, we need to be unwavering in our walk with God so that we can be blessed and bless others around us.

Key Verse
"I have been crucified with Christ and I no longer live, but Christ lives in me. The life I now live in the body, I live by faith in the Son of God, who loved me and gave himself for me."
Galatians 2:20 NIV

Bible Study
    Read Galatians 2:11-21.
    Who wrote the book of Galatians?
    Who is the author's original audience?
    When was the book written?

    Look at Galatians 2:11-14.
        What happened in verse 11? Who is Cephas?

        What did Paul do in verse 11? Why?
        Who did Cephas eat with in verse 12? Who are Gentiles?
        Who is in the "circumcision group"?

        Why did Paul call Cephas' actions hypocrisy in verse 13? Who joined in the hypocrisy? Who was led astray?

        What happened in verse 14? What did Paul say and do?

        Review the cross-references for more insight.
        Acts 10:28; 11:19-21; 13:39
        Galatians 2:1, 6-10
        Romans 1:1-5

    Look at Galatians 2:15-21 closely.
        How are God's people justified?

Since Christ came, is anyone justified by just following the law? Do people need circumcision?

What is Paul explaining in verses 17-18?

What does Paul say in verse 19?
What is the point Paul made in verse 20?

How does Paul reiterate his point in verse 21 concerning the works of the law? Once Christ came, how did things change?

Why should we be careful not to misrepresent the truth of Christ?

Review the cross-references for more insight.
Galatians 1:1-5; 3:21-22
Romans 7:4, 6:5-14; 8:37
2 Corinthians 5:15
1 Peter 4:2

Why was it important for Paul to respond to Peter concerning his behavior?

Can you think of a time when someone missed such an opportunity to share the truth with a fellow brother about his behavior?

Read other cross-references, commentaries, or use other Bible study tools as needed to consolidate your learning.

Reflection
How can I recognize when I need to stand up for God's truth?

Closing Prayer
Almighty God, I realize we all fall short of your glory. As flawed people we may sin intentionally or unintentionally. Forgive me of all my sins, known and unknown. As I read your word, help me internalize it and apply it as you instruct me. I want to stand up and abide in your truth. If I am not in your truth, then I am living a lie. Tell me when it is time to speak up and tell me when I must

remain silent. I do not want to lead anyone astray. As long as I am seeking you and your wisdom, give me strength to do what is right in your eyes. I have comfort in knowing you will provide the tools I need to live righteously. In the name of Jesus, Amen!

WEEK 12: ACTS OF LOVE

Key Question
How can I show love in action daily?

Opening Prayer
God, when you sent Jesus to us, you showed us love. Help me show your love to people. In the smallest of ways, show me how to reflect your light so that others may be transformed by your word. Thank you for salvation. In the name of Jesus, Amen!

Devotion
Think about the upcoming spring season. Animals begin to emerge from a period of hibernation and flowers begin to bloom. Everything seems to be fruitful and multiply! Insects contribute to the growth of flowers by the pollination process, and everyone's sinuses and asthma flare up! Spring is a great season that illustrates love through nature by what we see animals and plants do.

How can mankind show love? This may sound cliche, but it holds true that "actions speak louder than words." People may hear what you say, but they watch what you do. If you do not bear any fruit or have any works to accompany your actions, then does love exist?

Key Verse
"Love must be sincere. Hate what is evil; cling to what is good. Be devoted to one another in love. Honor one another above yourselves…"

Romans 12:9-10 NIV

Bible Study

Read Romans 12.
Who wrote the book of Romans?
Who is the author's original audience?
When was the book written?

Look at Romans 12:1-2.
What does Paul urge people to do in verse 1? Why?

What is Paul's warning in verse 2? What should we do instead? How is our mind renewed? If we renew our minds and are transformed, what is the benefit?

Review the cross-references for more insight.
Ephesians 4:1
Romans 6:13
1 Peter 1:14, 2:5
1 John 2:15

Look at Romans 12:3-8.
What does Paul say in verse 3?
What is Paul comparing in verses 4-5?

What does Paul say in verses 6-8? Why should people use the gifts God gave them as members of the body of Christ?

Review the cross-references for more insight.
Galatians 2:9
Ephesians 4:7
1 Corinthians 10:17; 12:4

Look at verses 9-21.
What does Paul say in verses 9-10?
What does Paul caution us about in verse 11? Who should we serve?

What does Paul say in verse 12?
What should we do in verse 13?

What are the instructions in verses 14-16?

Summarize the instructions in verses 17-21?

Why are these instructions important for Christian living?
What do these actions illustrate? Refer to verses 9-10.

Read the cross-references for more insight.

1 Timothy 1:5

Hebrews 13:1

Matthew 5:44

Philippians 2:3

What do acts of love look like?

Read other cross-references, commentaries, or use other Bible study tools as needed to consolidate your learning.

Reflection
How can I show love in action daily?

Closing Prayer

God, I understand I will never understand everything about you. However, thank you for speaking to my heart about love in your eyes. You give me just what I need to continue to do your will. I do not have to be a Bible scholar to be blessed by your word. All I need is to be a willing vessel. Help me show love the way you show love. Protect me during the week as I know the Devil will try to put out my light. As I walk in your favor, keep me close. In the name of Jesus, Amen!

WEEK 13: FIRST THINGS FIRST

Key Question
How does prioritizing and strengthening my relationship with God ensure I have all I need in life?

Opening Prayer
God, thank you for providing for me and the people I love. You know what I need before I ask. Help me seek your word and wisdom first. Your grace is sufficient. I can walk boldly because you are my God, and you are my guide. Prepare my heart for the word I will receive in this Bible study. In the name of Jesus, Amen!

Devotion
Well, winter is fading out and spring draws nearer. As spring approaches people may start reorganizing their wardrobe by placing winter clothes towards the back of the closet and finding clothes that are more comfortable for spring weather.

Spring sports will begin as parents scurry to sign up their children for youth sports leagues. Let's not forget that some adults play sports, too! There is nothing wrong with staying in physical shape. If anything, it is good for us adults! Furthermore, the weather may be more suitable for fishing and hunting. People assess the gear they have and may need to buy new gear or equipment. Either way, we start to prioritize things or see things from the perspective of spring, not winter.

As a new season of the year approaches, a new spiritual season may be approaching as well. Who knows what is to come in the next few weeks? Who knows what you may need if a crisis arises or if great celebrations are ahead of you? Maybe someone you know may have lost a job or is beginning a new career.

Maybe someone is waiting for a financial, physical, or mental breakthrough. Only God knows the current needs of his children and only God will supply them.

As you prepare physically, financially, or mentally for spring, ask God to prepare you spiritually with a heart posture towards him. In summary, seek God first in all your ways. If you do this, everything you need and more will be given to you no matter the season. Let go of everything, and let God do the work. You must have faith and be obedient. Father God is waiting for you to act on faith!

Key Verse
"'But seek first his kingdom and his righteousness, and all these things will be given to you as well."
Matthew 6:33 NIV

Bible Study
    Read Matthew 6:19-34
    Who wrote the Book of Matthew?
    Who is the author's original audience?
    When was the book written?

    Look at Matthew 6:19-24.
        Who is speaking in these verses?

        What is the warning about treasures stored on earth versus treasures stored in heaven? Review the cross-references for more insight.
        Proverbs 23:4-5
        Hebrews 13:5
        James 5:2-3
        Matthew 19:21
        Luke 12:33-34
        Luke 18:22
        1 Timothy 6:19

        How are your treasures and heart related according to verse 21?

What does verse 22 say about the health of your eyes and the connection to the health of your body? Is Jesus referring to physical health or spiritual health?

Why do you believe Jesus says your "eye is the lamp of the body"? Let the Holy Spirit guide you.

How does spiritual health relate to light and darkness?

What is the issue with serving two masters in verse 24? How does this relate to where you should store your treasures?

Look at Matthew 6:25-27.
What should you not worry about in verse 25? What should we focus on instead? Review the cross-references for more insight.
Luke 10:38-42
Luke 12:22-26
Philippians 4:4-9
1 Peter 5:7

What is said about birds in verse 26? Review the cross-references for more insight.
Job 38:4
Psalm 147:9
Matthew 10:29-31
Does God care for birds? How does God see you in comparison to birds? Is God in control of everything? Did he create everything?

In verse 27, why is worrying vain? Look at Psalms 39:4-6 for more insight.

Look at Matthew 6:28-34.
What does Jesus say in verses 28-32? What do pagans do? If one worries, what does it say about their faith?

What does Jesus tell you to focus on in verse 33? Why? Does

God know what you need?

How does the reading end in verse 34? Will God provide all you need and more? How do you know?

What is this reading clearly stating about who you should trust everyday of your life?

Read other cross-references, commentaries, or use other Bible study tools as needed to consolidate your learning.

Reflection

How does prioritizing and strengthening my relationship with God ensure I have all I need in life?

Closing Prayer

Lord, thank you for showing me that you are all I need this winter season and for all seasons to come. If I have you, I have everything I need. If my family and friends have you, they have everything they need. May I live my life with spiritual eyes that desire only you. You are worthy of all my attention. If I seek you first, I will live a prosperous and fulfilling life. Additionally, I will be sufficient for all the people who depend on me. May I lead my family and teach them to seek you first. May we experience pure joy now and in our future. Thank you for showing me that I will always be enough because you are more than enough. In the name of Jesus, Amen!

SEE YOU NEXT SEASON

Greetings Brother in Christ,

Prayerfully, these devotions and Bible studies have blessed you as much as it has blessed us, the authors. Making connections across Bible studies over the weeks help solidify and reiterate the goodness of God. God can work through us in unimaginable ways. We must believe it can happen!

God loves us so much that he made us in his image and sent his son to save us. Therefore, we must be holy and blameless before him. We can become holy through the process of sanctification. The wonderful news is that God's word sanctifies us. When we read, study, and apply God's word, we bless ourselves and everyone in our circle. Demons must flee, and we are protected by an almighty, loving Father.

I pray you were able to stay warm and secure this cold winter season with the word of God. Now, let's spring into the next season. Pun intended!

Your Brothers in Christ,

Jarome and Mark

BOOKS IN THIS SERIES

God in Seasons for Men is a collection of four books for men to experience God in all seasons of the year. Each book has 13 devotions and Bible studies for each season.

Books are available in eBook and paperback formats. Additionally, each book has a paperback notebook, which makes a great companion to the book. These notebooks are perfect for jotting notes, special thoughts, scriptures, and prayers. View the author profile on amazon for more details about books at https://www.amazon.com/author/beinspiredbygod.

God in the Winter: 13 Bible Studies & Devotions for Men

Available for purchase.

God in the Spring: 13 Bible Studies & Devotions for Men

Coming in February 2024.

God in the Summer: 13 Bible Studies & Devotions for Men

Coming in April 2024.

God in the Fall: 13 Bible Studies & Devotions for Men

Coming August 2024.

ACKNOWLEDGEMENTS

We acknowledge all our family and friends who support this book. It was written by ordinary people who believe in an extraordinary God. Thank you for believing and thank you for your prayers.

Made in the USA
Columbia, SC
17 March 2025